The Countries

Somalia

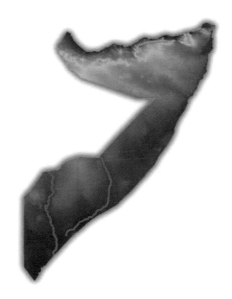

Tamara L. Britton
ABDO Publishing Company

visit us at
www.abdopub.com

Published by ABDO Publishing Company, 4940 Viking Drive, Edina, Minnesota 55435.
Copyright © 2003 by Abdo Consulting Group, Inc. International copyrights reserved in
all countries. No part of this book may be reproduced in any form without written
permission from the publisher.

Printed in the United States.

Photo Credits: Corbis, AP/Wide World
Contributing Editors: Kristin Van Cleaf, Stephanie Hedlund
Art Direction & Maps: Neil Klinepier
Special thanks to Yasin Elmi Garad for his help with the Somali language.

Library of Congress Cataloging-in-Publication Data

Britton, Tamara L., 1963-
  Somalia / Tamara L. Britton.
     p. cm. -- (The countries)
  Includes index.
  Summary: An introduction to the history, geography, economy, government, people,
and more of the east African country of Somalia.
  ISBN 1-57765-844-2
     1. Somalia--Juvenile literature. [1. Somalia.] I. Title. II. Series.

DT401.5 .B75 2002
967.73--dc21

                                                       2002020791

Contents

Hayeh!

Hello from Somalia! Somalia is a country in east Africa. It occupies the land known as the Horn of Africa. Somalia is a land of rugged mountains and hot deserts. It is home to many plants and animals.

Most of Somalia's people are **nomads**. They live in movable shelters and travel to find food for their animals. Almost all Somalis (so-MAH-lees) speak Somali and practice Islam. But they are fiercely divided among clans.

Somalia has suffered through many years of **civil war**. Fighting between rival clans has destroyed its government. Many Somalis have moved to other countries. In 2000, Somalian leaders came together to form a new government. These leaders are working hard to rebuild Somalia for its people.

Hayeh *from Somalia!*

Fast Facts

OFFICIAL NAME: Somalia (Soomaaliya)
CAPITAL: Mogadishu

LAND
- Area: 246,201 square miles (637,657 sq km)
- Highest Point: Surud Cad 7,900 feet (2,408 m)
- Lowest Point: Indian Ocean (sea level)
- Major Rivers: Jubba, Shabeelle

PEOPLE
- Population: 8,788,000 (2000 UN est.)
- Major Cities: Mogadishu, Marca
- Languages: Somali, Arabic, Italian, English
- Religion: Islam

GOVERNMENT
- Form: Transitional National Government
- Head of State: President
- Head of Government: Prime minister
- Legislature: National Assembly
- Flag: Light blue field with white five-pointed star in center
- Nationhood: July 1, 1960

ECONOMY
- Agricultural Products: Bananas, sorghum, corn, sugarcane, mangoes, sesame seeds, beans; cattle, sheep, goats, fish
- Mining Products: None
- Manufactured Products: Textiles, leather goods
- Money: Somali shilling (1 shilling = 100 cents)

MOGADISHU

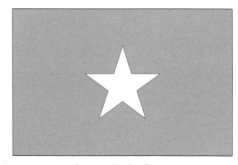

Somalia's flag

Timeline

A.D. 800s	Muslim Arabs develop trading posts along the Indian Ocean
900s	Muslim Arabs live along the coast; Somalian nomads live inland
1884	Britain creates British Somaliland
1889	Italy creates Italian Somaliland
1900s	Maxamed Cabdulle Xasan protests British rule
1950	Italian Somaliland becomes a UN trust territory
1960	British and Italian Somaliland unite to form the independent Republic of Somalia
1969	Major General Maxamed Siyaad Barre leads military coup; creates socialist Somali Democratic Republic
1991	United Somali Congress forces Barre from power
1992-1995	UN attempts peacekeeping mission; fighting continues
2000	Somalian leaders create the Transitional National Government, expected to rule for three years

History

In ancient times, parts of Somalia formed the land of Punt. Around the ninth century A.D., Muslim Arabs moved into Somalia's land. They developed trading posts along the Gulf of Aden and the Indian Ocean. By the tenth century, Muslim Arabs lived along the coasts. Somalian **nomads** lived inland.

In 1839, the British took control of Aden. They set up a **protectorate** in 1884. They named it British Somaliland. In 1889, Italy took control of two protectorates in northern Somalia, and one along the southern coast. The Italians called these areas Italian Somaliland.

A stone carving of people traveling to the ancient land of Punt

In the early 1900s, Maxamed Cabdulle Xasan
(ma-HAH-mad ab-DOOL HA-sahn) brought many
Muslim Somalis together to fight against British rule.
The British defeated them in 1920.

In 1936, Italy conquered Ethiopia. Italian Somaliland
and Ethiopia became states in the Italian East African
Empire. In 1940, the Italians captured British Somaliland.
But in 1941, the British gained control of both British
and Italian Somaliland, and freed Ethiopia.

In 1950, Italian Somaliland
became a **United Nations
(UN) trust territory**. The
UN decided that Somalia
was to be independent
within 10 years. During this
time, Somalis in British
Somaliland demanded the
right to govern themselves.

*Rodolfo Graziani, governor
of Italian Somaliland*

*President
Maxamed Siyaad Barre*

So in 1960, Italian and British Somaliland united to form the independent **Republic** of Somalia. The people elected a president and **prime minister**.

In the 1960s, some Somalis still lived in parts of Ethiopia, Kenya, and present-day Djibouti (juh-BOO-tee). Some people wanted to include these areas in Somalia. But the countries fought against this control.

In 1967, the people elected Abdi Rashid Ali Sharmaarke (ABDIH RASH-id alih SHAR-mahrk) as their president. Maxamed Xaaji Ibrahiim Cigaal (ma-HAH-mad HAHJIH ih-bra-HEEM ih-GAHL) was prime minister. The government restored peace between the fighting countries. But many Somalis believed this new government did not treat the clans equally.

In 1969, Sharmaarke was **assassinated**. The government then fell during a military **coup** (KOO) led by Major General Maxamed Siyaad Barre (ma-HAH-mad SIH-ahd BARR). Barre, along with the Supreme

Revolutionary Council, created the Somali **Democratic Republic**.

Barre soon made many changes. He declared Somalia a **socialist** state. The new government outlawed clan loyalties. In 1973 and 1974, **literacy** programs helped make Somali a written language for the first time.

In 1977, Somalia invaded the Ogaden (oh-GAH-dayn) region of Ethiopia. The goal was to unite this **ethnic** Somali area with Somalia. The invasion did not succeed. Ethiopia reconquered the Ogaden in 1978. Thousands of Ogaden Somali fled to Somalia.

In 1991, the United Somali Congress, a **rebel** group of many clans, forced Barre from power. But the Congress again broke into clan groups.

Two of the main groups were led by Maxamed Farax Caydiid

*Maxamed Farax Caydiid (left)
and Cali Mahdi Maxamed*

(ma-HAH-mad far-AH aye-DEED) and Cali Mahdi Maxamed (alih MAH-dih ma-HAH-mad). The two groups fought, destroying much of the capital. Another **rebel** group, called the Somali National Movement, declared northern Somalia an independent nation. They called it the Somaliland **Republic**.

Continued fighting between rival clans upset Somalia's government and **economy**. Thousands of Somalis died in the fighting. Others died of starvation. Because of these hardships, many Somalis fled to other countries.

In 1992, **UN** forces attempted to stop the fighting. They tried to distribute food and supplies to the suffering Somalian people. But the clan leaders fought against the UN forces. The clans often stole the food and supplies before they could be given to the people.

In 1993, clan leader Maxamed Farax Caydiid said that UN officials were favoring other clans over his. That June, his clan forces killed many UN peacekeepers. The UN fought back by bombing Caydiid's headquarters.

In 1994 and 1995, **UN** troops left Somalia. About this time, Caydiid named himself president. But the clans continued to fight. He died in 1996, and his son Husein (HUH-sehn) Caydiid took his place.

In 2000, a group of Somalian leaders created the Transitional National Government. They elected a National Assembly, which elected Abdiqassim Salad Hassan (ab-DIH-ka-sihm sa-LAHD hah-SAHN) Somalia's president. Abdiqassim appointed Ali Khalif Galaydh (alih KHAH-lihf GAHL-ihd) as **prime minister**, who set up a **cabinet**. This government was set to govern for three years.

Husein Caydiid took over as his clan's leader after his father's death.

In October of 2001, the National Assembly voted Ali Khalif Galaydh from office. In November, it replaced him with Hassan Abshir Farar (hahs-SAHN ab-SHIHR far-AHR). The new **prime minister** set up a new **cabinet**. He said unifying the Somalian people was his top priority.

Many years of fighting between clans has destroyed Somalia's government, **economy**, and **infrastructure**. Thousands of Somalis have died from war and starvation. Many others have fled Somalia and **immigrated** to other countries. Somalia's temporary government has a tough challenge ahead. It is working to make Somalia a better place for its people.

President
Abdiqassim Salad Hassan

Somalia's Land

Somalia is bounded on the north by the Gulf of Aden. To the east lies the Indian Ocean, and to the west are Kenya and Ethiopia. On the northwest, Somalia shares a border with Djibouti.

In the north lies the Guban coastal **plain**. The Galgodon Highlands rise from the plain. South of the highlands lies the flat Hawd **Plateau** (plah-TOH). Below the plateau, Somalia is a flat, grassy plain that leads to the Indian Ocean.

The Jubba (JOO-buh) and Shabeelle (sha-BAY-leh) Rivers flow across Somalia from Ethiopia to the Indian Ocean. These rivers are the main source of water for **irrigation**. Many of Somalia's farms are along these rivers.

Somalia has a mostly desert climate. The country has two rainy seasons and two dry seasons. The *gu* (GOO) rainy season is from March to May, and the *dayr* (DIER) is

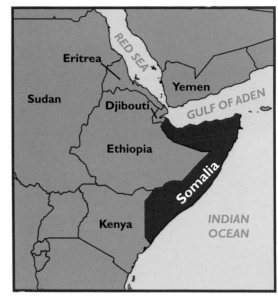

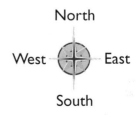

from October to December. The north is drier than the south. But even in the wetter southern region, it rarely rains more than 20 inches (51 cm) a year.

Dry monsoon winds blow during the dry seasons. The *jiilaal* (jee-LAHL) season is from December to February. The *xaggaa* (HAG-ah) is from May to October. Droughts are common during these seasons. But some rain falls on the coast during the *xaggaa*.

Monsoon winds can cause dust storms during Somalia's dry seasons.

Rainfall

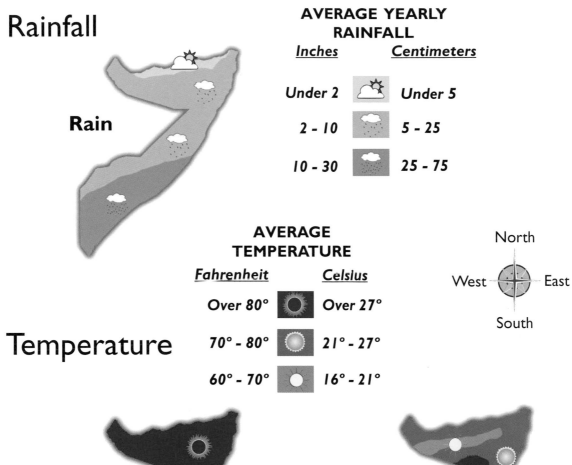

Rain

AVERAGE YEARLY RAINFALL

Inches		*Centimeters*
Under 2		Under 5
2 - 10		5 - 25
10 - 30		25 - 75

AVERAGE TEMPERATURE

Fahrenheit		*Celsius*
Over 80°		Over 27°
70° - 80°		21° - 27°
60° - 70°		16° - 21°

North
West — East
South

Temperature

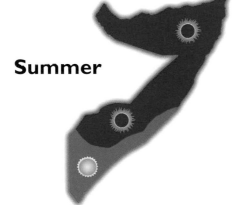

Summer

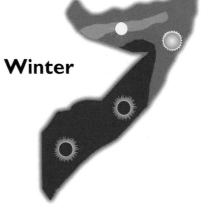

Winter

Plants & Animals

Somalia's plant and animal life varies by region. Dry, grassy **plains** cover most of the land. Wide areas of grass and thorny shrubs cover the northern **plateaus**. But the northern coastal plain has little vegetation.

Thornbush and cacti grow in the south and northwest. Aloes, baobabs, and incense trees grow in the drier areas. Thorny acacia (uh-KAY-shuh) trees and shrubs blossom with yellow or white flowers. Along the rivers, mangrove, kapock, and papaya trees grow well.

Somalia's lands are home to many animals, too. They include lions, elephants, hyenas, foxes, leopards, giraffes, zebras, and antelope. Many beautiful birds also live on these lands. They include herons, partridge, guinea fowl, green pigeons, and ostrich.

A giraffe eats from an acacia tree.

Somalia's People

Somalia's many different groups share a language, **culture**, and religion. But they are divided by fierce loyalty to their clans.

Many Somalis are settled herdsmen. They belong to two clans that together are called the Saab. Many of these people live in villages grouped along the rivers.

Most other Somalis are **nomads**. They belong to four clans that together are called the Samaal. Somalian nomads live in *aqal* (AK-ahl). These homes are dome-shaped frames covered with woven grass mats. The nomads can take these houses with them as they travel.

Almost all Somalis practice the religion of Sunni (SUH-nee) Islam. Somali is the official language, but some Somalis also speak Arabic, Italian, or English. Many Somalis wear traditional clothing consisting of brightly-colored cloth draped around the body. Most urban Somalis wear clothing similar to that of Americans or Europeans.

Somalis eat whatever they produce. Those that live near the water eat more seafood. **Nomads** drink goat milk and eat goat and camel meat. Farmers eat more fruits and grains.

A nomadic woman ties grass mats to the wooden frame of her aqal.

Somalian children attend **Koranic** schools. They teach about religion, customs, and ethics. Children must also attend elementary school.

Beyond elementary school, education is not required. If they choose, students may study at Somalia National University in Mogadishu (mah-guh-DIH-shoo), or at **vocational** or agricultural secondary schools. But less than one-fifth of Somalian children attend school. Most Somalis cannot read or write.

Due to decades of **civil war**, conditions in Somalia are poor. Much of the country's **infrastructure** has been destroyed. Most Somalis only make enough money to survive. Many Somalis do not have a place to live, or enough to eat.

A Somalian boy holds up a Koran board. The board includes verses from the Koran, the Muslim holy book.

Somali Flatbread

Somali Flatbread is a traditional Somalian food.

- 2 cups self-rising flour
- 1 egg
- 1 cup water
- 1 teaspoon oil

Preheat frying pan over medium heat. Mix all ingredients together in a bowl. Add a little oil to the pan. Add 1/3 cup of batter to the pan, tilting the pan so the batter covers the bottom. Cook covered for 3 to 5 minutes. Remove flatbread from pan. Repeat until all the batter is used.

AN IMPORTANT NOTE TO THE CHEF: Always have an adult help with the preparation and cooking of food. Never use kitchen utensils or appliances without adult permission and supervision.

LANGUAGE

English	Somali
Yes	Haye (hi-AY)
No	Maya (MYAH)
Thank you	Mahadsanid (mah-HAHD-sah-nihd)
Please	Fadlan (FAHD-lahn)
Hello	Hayeh (hi-EH)
Good-bye	Nabadeey (nahbah-DAY)

Making a Living

Somalia is a developing country with limited resources. Its **economy** is based on agriculture and the raising of livestock.

Only about two percent of Somalia's land is fit to grow crops. Still, many Somalis earn their living by farming. Farmers grow citrus fruits and bananas along the Jubba and Shabeelle Rivers. They also grow sugarcane, sorghum, and corn. Some raise livestock as well.

A large percentage of Somalis are **nomads**. They earn their living by raising livestock. They herd sheep, goats, camels, and cattle across the dry land, looking for food and water.

Industry has been damaged by the **civil war**. So industry in Somalia is small. It consists of meat and fish processing, and **textile** and leather manufacturing.

Opposite page: A Somalian nomad loads items onto a camel. In Somalia, camels have many uses. They provide food, trade, and transportation. These animals are important to the nomadic way of life.

As a result of its developing **economy**, Somalia imports more than it exports. Somalia imports **petroleum** products, food, and construction materials. It exports livestock, bananas, hides, and fish. Somalia's major trade partners are Djibouti, Kenya, Brazil, and Saudi Arabia.

Somalian Cities

Mogadishu is Somalia's capital and largest city. It is also Somalia's commercial and financial center. Mogadishu is located just north of the equator, along the Indian Ocean.

Arabs created Mogadishu in the tenth century as a trading center. It was the capital of Italian Somaliland, and became independent Somalia's capital in 1960.

Somalia National University and the National Museum are in Mogadishu's Garesa Palace. The Garesa Palace was built in the nineteenth century by the Sultan of Zanzibar. Fakr ad-Din, a thirteenth-century **mosque** (MAHSK), is also in Mogadishu. Somalia's **civil war** has resulted in widespread destruction of the city.

Marca is a Somalian city along the coast. It is about 45 miles (72 km) south of Mogadishu. The city was a

Opposite page: The fighting in Mogadishu has damaged much of the city. Despite this damage, many people still live there. They hope they will be able to rebuild some day.

trading center in the tenth century. Somalian **ethnic** groups arrived in the thirteenth century.

Marca is a port on the Indian Ocean. However, large coral reefs prevent ships from coming close to shore. Small boats take goods between the oceangoing ships and the shore.

Transportation

Somalia has about 13,733 miles (22,100 km) of roads. But only about 1,620 miles (2,608 km) of these roads are paved. During the rainy seasons, many rural areas cannot be reached by motor vehicles because of muddy roads.

Less than one percent of all Somalis own a car. Within the country, most people travel by truck. Buses also run between the big cities.

Mogadishu International Airport is four miles (six km) west of Mogadishu. Somali Airlines is the country's national airline. There are no railways.

Somalia has one daily newspaper, which is published in the Somali language. Other papers are published in Arabic, Italian, and English. The country also has two radio stations.

Motor vehicles and good roads are not available in all parts of Somalia. Instead, many rural Somali use animals such as camels or donkeys for transportation. These men use a donkey and cart to haul water from a river.

Forming a Government

Somalia became an independent nation on July 1, 1960. Since then, it has largely been a **republic**.

The **constitution** of 1979 gave executive power to a president, and legislative power to an elected People's Assembly. Somalia does not have an independent judicial system. The country's laws are based on Islamic law. But Somalis often have more loyalty to their clan than to their country. So Somalia has not had a stable, **democratic** government.

In 1991, a **rebel** group called the United Somali Congress overthrew the government. The rebels took control of the government and appointed a president and a **cabinet**. But the United Somali Congress then broke up into smaller clan groups, which fought against each other. Somalia was left with no government at all.

In 2000, a group that included Somalian clan leaders elected the National Assembly. The Assembly's 245 members elected a new president. The president appointed a **prime minister**, who set up a 25-member **cabinet**. This temporary government's goal was to create a permanent **constitution** within three years.

Kenyan president Daniel Arap Moi (center) meets with Somalian prime minister Hassan Abshir Farar (left) and Puntland leader Jami Ali Jama (right) at a peace conference in Nakuru, Kenya, in December of 2001. The men hope to work out a permanent government for Somalia.

Holidays & Festivals

Somalis celebrate both religious and national holidays. Because Somalia has changed hands many times in its long history, Somalis observe two independence days. In the north, Independence Day is on June 26. But the whole country celebrates its independence on July 1.

Because most Somalis practice Islam, they also celebrate Islamic holidays. Most Somalis observe Ramadan. During Ramadan, Muslims do not eat, drink, or smoke between sunrise and sunset.

At the end of Ramadan, another of Islam's great celebrations, Eid-ul-Fitr, ends the great fast. During this holiday, Muslims feast and show goodwill to the poor.

Opposite page: The Somali sing and dance to celebrate many of their festivals and holidays. For example, Somalis often dance for a week after a marriage. These women dance and sing in support of a separate government for Somaliland.

Somalian Culture

The telling of sayings, stories, and poems is an important part of Somalian **culture**. Somali was an unwritten language until 1973. Somalian culture had to be remembered and told to others. Today, the Somalian people have a rich tradition of oral literature.

Stories and **folktales** are a large part of the oral tradition. At the end of the day, Somalis often gather together to share stories. These stories usually teach lessons as well as entertain.

Poetry is also important in the oral tradition. Somalis memorize many poems and recite them to others. Common subjects in Somalian poetry are war, peace, women, horses, and camels.

Opposite page: Somalis gather to listen to each other speak. Being able to speak well is highly respected in Somalian society. People often use this ability to tell proverbs. These sayings usually tell a truth about how people live or the way things are. Humor is also highly valued in Somalian oral culture.

Sometimes poetry takes the form of a song. Somalis sing for different reasons. Often they sing while working or doing chores.

Some Somalis have brought their poetry traditions to the rest of the world. Maxamed Cabdulle Xasan is a famous Somalian poet. Nuuradiin Farah (NOO-rah-deen FAR-ah) has written works in English.

Glossary

assassinate - to murder an important or famous person, usually for political reasons.

cabinet - a group of advisers chosen by the prime minister to lead government departments.

civil war - a war between groups in the same country.

constitution - the laws that govern a country.

coup - a sudden overthrow of an established government.

culture - the customs, arts, and tools of a nation or people at a certain time.

democracy - a governmental system in which the people vote on how to run the country.

economy - the way a nation uses its money, goods, and natural resources.

ethnic - a way to describe a group of people who are of the same race, nationality, or culture.

folktale - stories that are part of the beliefs, traditions, and customs of a people. Folktales are handed down from parent to child.

immigrate - to enter another country to live.

infrastructure - the basic framework of public society, including its government, economy, transportation, and schools.

irrigate - to supply land with water by using channels, streams, or pipes.

Koran - the sacred book of Islam. It contains Islam's religious and moral code. Muslims believe the Koran is the word of Allah, as revealed by the archangel Gabriel to the Prophet Muhammad.

literacy - being able to read and write.

mosque - a Muslim place of worship.

nomad - a member of a tribe that moves from place to place in search of food or pasture for its animals.

petroleum - a thick, yellowish-black oil. It is the source of gasoline.

plain - a flat stretch of land.

plateau - a raised area of flat land.

prime minister - the highest-ranked member of some governments.

protectorate - a government set up by a strong country to control an area of weaker power.

rebel - to disobey an authority or the government.

republic - a form of government in which authority rests with voting citizens and is carried out by elected officials such as a parliament.

socialism - a type of economy. The government or citizens control the production and distribution of goods.

textile - of or having to do with the designing, manufacturing, or producing of woven fabric.

trust territory - a territory without its own government put under the authority of another government by the United Nations.

United Nations (UN) - a group of nations formed in 1945. Its goals are peace, human rights, security, and social and economic development.

vocational - of or relating to training in a skill or trade to be pursued as a career.

Web Sites

Would you like to learn more about Somalia? Please visit **www.abdopub.com** to find up-to-date Web site links about Somalia's people, oral culture, and land. These links are routinely monitored and updated to provide the most current information available.

Index